DISCOVER THE DIFFERENCE

Bat and Bird

Rod Theodorou and Carole Telford

RIGBY
INTERACTIVE
LIBRARY

This edition © 1997 Rigby Education
Published by Rigby Interactive Library,
an imprint of Rigby Education,
division of Reed Elsevier, Inc.
500 Coventry Lane
Crystal Lake, IL 60014

Printed in Britain

Library of Congress Cataloging-in-Publication Data
Theodorou, Rod.
        Bat and bird / Rod Theodorou and Carole Telford.
            p.   cm. — (Discover the difference)
        Summary: Compares and contrasts the physical attributes, habits,
    and habitat of bats and birds.
        Includes index.
        ISBN 1-57572-104-X
        1. Bats—Juvenile literature. 2. Birds—Juvenile literature. [1. Bats. 2. Birds.]
    I. Telford, Carole, 1961– . II. Title. III. Series: Theodorou, Rod. Discover the difference.
    QL737.C5T48 1996
    598—dc20   96-7237

Designed by Susan Clarke
Illustrations by Adam Abel

Acknowledgments
The publisher would like to thank the following for permission to reproduce photographs: Nigel
Tucker/Planet Earth Pictures, p. 4; Hans Reinhard/Oxford Scientific Films, p. 5 *left*; Kevin Schafer/NHPA,
p. 5 *right*, John Downer/Planet Earth Pictures, p. 6 *top*; Hans and Judy Beste/ Ardea London Ltd., pp. 3
top, 6 *bottom*, 12 *bottom*; Yuri Shibnev/Planet Earth Pictures, p. 7; Stephen Dalton/NHPA, pp. 8, 16
bottom; Oxford Scientific Films, p. 14; Gerard Lacz/NHPA, p. 9; I.R. Beames/Ardea London Ltd., p. 10;
R. de la Harpe/Planet Earth Pictures, p. 11 *top*; Mary Clay/Planet Earth Pictures, p. 11 *bottom*; Merlin
Tuttle/Oxford Scientific Films, pp. 12 *top*, 16 *top*; A. Wharton/FLPA, p. 13 *top*; Robert Tyrrell/Oxford
Scientific Films, pp. 3 *bottom*, 13 *bottom*; K. Ammann/Planet Earth Pictures, p. 15 *top*; Jan Johansson/
Planet Earth Pictures, p. 15 *bottom*; R.A. Austing/FLPA, p. 17; ANT/NHPA, p. 18; Ken Lucas/Planet
Earth Pictures, p. 19; Ardea London Ltd., p. 20; Michael Habicht/Oxford Scientific Films, p. 21 *top*;
Melvin Grey/NHPA, p. 21 *bottom*; Stephen Krasemann/NHPA, p. 22; David Hosking/FLPA, p. 23.

Cover photographs reproduced with permission of Oxford Scientific Films, *top*;
Melvin Grey/NHPA , *bottom*.

Every effort has been made to contact copyright holders of any material reproduced in this book.
Any omissions will be rectified in subsequent printings if notice is given to the publisher.

Note to the Reader
Some words in this book are printed in **bold** type. This indicates that the word is
listed in the glossary on page 24. The glossary gives a brief explanation of words
that may be new to you and tells you the page on which the word first appears.

Contents

Introduction

Only three kinds of animals can fly—bats, birds, and insects. Bats are the only **mammals** that can fly. There are more than 950 **species**, or kinds, of bat. They have small furry bodies and two leathery wings. Most bats are nocturnal, or active at night. They sleep during the day and feed when the sun goes down.

It's amazing!
Most bats have tiny, weak legs. They can only crawl on the ground.

Bats look graceful when they fly but not when they stop.

Starlings are one of the most common birds in the world.

Penguins have thick feathers to protect them from the cold of the Antarctic.

There are about 8,700 species of birds. Birds are the only animals that grow feathers to keep themselves warm and dry. Birds have beaks, wings, and strong legs for holding onto branches or hopping along the ground. Some birds, like ostriches, emus, and penguins, cannot fly.

Habitat

Bats live in many parts of the world. They sleep in places where they will not be disturbed during the day. They **roost** in caves, trees, and old buildings. Bats that live in cooler countries **hibernate** during the winter. Many types of bat are becoming rarer because their **habitats** are being destroyed.

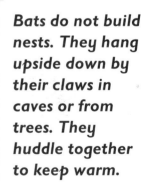

Bats do not build nests. They hang upside down by their claws in caves or from trees. They huddle together to keep warm.

It's amazing!

When the weather turns cool, some bats migrate to warmer countries. They may travel more than 620 miles!

Birds live all over the world, from frozen Antarctica to dry, hot deserts and tropical rain forests. Birds migrate to take advantage of the seasons and the best supplies of food. They return to their breeding grounds in the spring and migrate again when the weather grows cold. More then 1,000 species of bird are in danger of **extinction** because of pollution, hunting, or the destruction of their habitats.

The golden eagle can make a nest as wide as a car!

Wonderful Wings

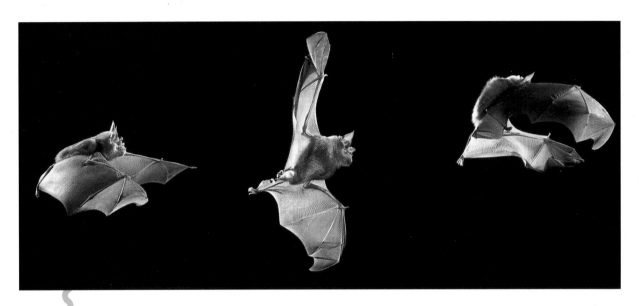

A bat in flight.

Bats fly with their hands! They have long arms and very long finger bones. Thin elastic skin grows across these bones, like fabric stretched across the rods of an umbrella. The thumb is short and has a useful claw that helps the bat grip its food or crawl. Bats have strong chest and shoulder muscles to help them fly.

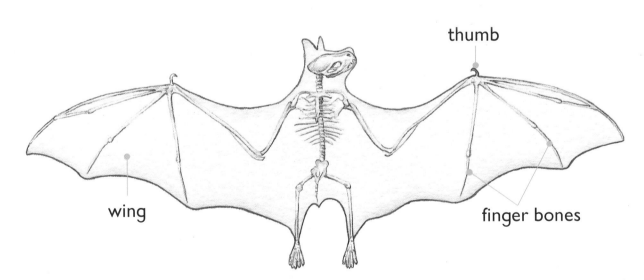

thumb

wing

finger bones

The skeleton of a bat.

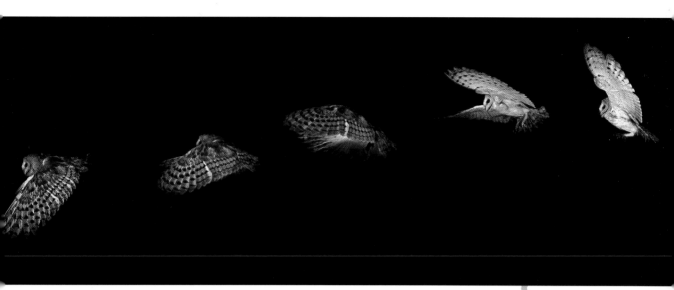

Like bats, birds fly very fast. Their wings are curved on top and flat underneath, like the wings of a plane. The bones of most birds are hollow and light. They have a large breastbone and powerful chest muscles to help them fly. Small birds can flap their wings quickly and twist and turn through the trees. Large birds can spread their wings and, with the help of powerful air currents, soar over mountains and oceans.

It's amazing!

Birds' feathers are made from keratin, the same material as your hair and nails.

An owl in flight.

The skeleton of a bird.

wing

breastbone

Senses

Some people think that bats are blind. This is not true. Bats have good eyesight. However, because they are nocturnal, they must be able to fly and catch **prey** in total darkness. To do this, they have developed **echolocation**. The bat makes rapid high-pitched squeaks. The sounds bounce off objects and echo back to the bat. Different objects make different echoes. By listening to the echoes, bats can even find and catch flying insects in the dark.

It's amazing!

Many insect-eating bats have huge ears to help them hear echoes. The long-eared bat's ears are almost as long as its body!

Most fruit bats do not use echolocation. This bat uses its big eyes and long nose to find ripe fruit and flowers.

Birds have a poor sense of smell but good eyesight. Eagles and hawks have eyesight twice as good as ours, which helps them spot small animals below them as they fly. Most birds have good hearing and often sing to let other birds know where they are. Birds also sing to attract mates. At breeding time, some birds sing their song more than a thousand times a day!

A vulture looks for dead or dying animals to feed on.

Owls need good eyesight and hearing to catch mice rustling through the grass at night.

Plant Eaters

This fruit bat is eating bananas.

A lesser long-nosed bat is about to feed.

Fruit-eating bats are often called *flying foxes*. They live only in hot countries. Bats eat fruits such as bananas, mangoes, and guavas. They also lick **nectar** and **pollen** from flowers. Sometimes pollen sticks on their fur and gets carried to other flowers. In this way, bats pollinate flowers, helping new plants to grow. Fruit bats help fruit trees grow, too. Bats spit out seeds or spread seeds in their droppings.

Many birds eat fruit, seeds, or other plants. Seed-eating birds often have strong beaks for opening nuts and pine cones. Birds that eat water plants usually have flat bills, like ducks. Many plant-eating birds live in towns and cities and find their food in gardens or parks.

Starlings are very common birds. They eat fruit, insects, and seeds.

It's amazing!

Hummingbirds are the smallest birds. They have thin bills and long tongues that they use like a straw to suck nectar from flowers.

Insect Eaters

Most bats eat insects. Using echolocation, they find moths, gnats, mosquitoes, and other insects. Bats catch insects in their mouths or scoop them up in the flap of skin between their legs, or in their wings. Some bats even pluck spiders off their webs.

A greater horseshoe bat is chasing a moth.

Insect-eating birds often have thin, pointed beaks. Some catch insects in the air. Others look on the ground or on the bark of trees to find hidden grubs or beetles. Bee-eaters catch bees and squeeze out the bee's stinger before eating the bee. Flamingos' long legs allow them to hunt in deep water without wetting their feathers.

A flamingo feeds on creatures found in shallow water.

This nuthatch is looking for beetles and earwigs in the tree bark.

15

Meat Eaters

A fisherman bat catches a fish.

Some bats use echolocation to catch fish! When a small fish swims close to the surface of the water, fish-eating bats detect the ripples and swoop down to catch the fish. Other big bats, like the false vampire bat, eat frogs, rodents, lizards, small birds, and even other bats.

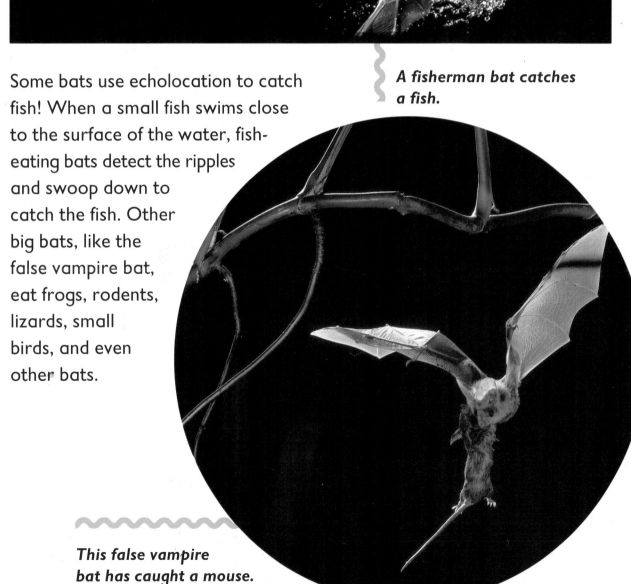

This false vampire bat has caught a mouse.

Fish-eating birds, like herons and kingfishers, have sharp bills to stab their prey. Birds of prey, like eagles, hawks, and owls, have huge, hooked claws and beaks for gripping and tearing flesh. The African harrier hawk has especially flexible legs to help it reach into holes in trees and grab nesting birds or bats.

A saw-whet owl swoops to catch a mouse.

Babies

Female bats look for a warm, dry roost when it is time to have their babies. Thousands of females huddle together in the same place, often giving birth at exactly the same time. Most bats have only one baby a year. Insect-eating bats are born blind and bald. Fruit bats are born with their eyes open.

Eastern horseshoe bats hang out in a nursery roost.

Most birds build a nest in which to lay the eggs. Some birds lay just one egg. Others can lay as many as nineteen. The parents sit on the eggs to keep them warm until they hatch—this is called **incubation.** Some birds' eggs need about 11 days to hatch, while others need up to 85 days.

Chicks are born with a special "egg-tooth" to help them break out of their egg.

Growing Up

If their roost is disturbed, mother bats fly off with their babies clinging to their fur.

Mother bats feed their babies milk. When the mother flies off to find food, the babies huddle together to keep warm. After one to three months, the baby bats are ready to fly. Young bats have to practice echolocation and sometimes fly behind their mother to learn how to hunt.

It's amazing!

To practice flying, baby fruit bats sometimes hang from branches and flap their wings!

Baby birds are called *nestlings*. The nestlings' parents fly off and hunt for food for them until the babies learn to fly. Birds that are old enough to fly from the nest and learn to feed themselves are called *fledglings*. Many clumsy fledglings are caught by birds of prey.

Nestlings open their mouths wide to show their parents that they're hungry.

A barn owl brings a rabbit home for its young.

Fact File

Bat

Largest
The wingspan of a Bismark flying fox is as long as 6 feet—as long as some grownups are tall.

Smallest
Kitti's hog-nosed bat has a wingspan of only 6 inches.

Fastest
The Mexican free-tailed bat can fly at 60 mph.

Food
Plant-eating bats eat fruit, pollen, and nectar.

Insect-eating bats eat gnats, moths, mosquitoes, dragonflies, crickets, grasshoppers, and spiders.

Meat-eating bats eat frogs, fish, rodents, birds, and other bats.

A colony of bats roosts in Bracken Cave, Texas.

Life Span
Most bats live from 5 to 20 years. There is a record of a banded little brown bat living to the age of 32.

Largest Colony
One colony of Mexican free-tailed bats in Bracken Cave, Texas, was estimated to have 20 million bats in one cave!

Bird

The ostrich is one of the species of bird which cannot fly.

Largest
The ostrich can grow up to 9 feet tall and weigh 345 pounds.

The largest flying birds are bustards, which can weigh up to 46 pounds.

The albatross has the longest wing span—up to 11 feet 11 inches.

Smallest
The bee hummingbird is only 2.24 inches long and weighs 0.056 ounce.

Fastest Moving
The peregrine falcon can dive at speeds of up to 112 mph.

Food
Some birds eat only seeds, fruit, or insects. Some, such as crows, also eat worms and dead meat. Many seabirds eat mainly fish. Small birds of prey catch mice and other small animals. The biggest birds of prey will catch animals as big as a young deer.

Life Span
"Cocky," a cockatoo at London Zoo, lived for 80 years.

Largest Colony
In the winter of 1951–52, an estimated 70 million bramblings gathered every night near Hunibach, Switzerland.

Glossary

echolocation a process that allows bats to locate prey. Sound   10
waves are bounced off the prey and echo back to the bat.

extinction the condition in which all the animals of a species   7
die out

habitat the place in which an animal lives   6

hibernate to sleep through winter   6

incubation the period during which birds keep eggs warm   19
by sitting on them

mammals fur-covered animals that feed their young milk   4

migrate to move from one area to another each year   6

nectar a sweet liquid-like honey that some plants make to   12
attract birds, bats, and insects

pollen tiny yellow grains produced by the male parts of plants   12
which fertilize the female parts of plants

prey an animal that is hunted by another animal for food   10

roost the place where a flying animal sleeps   6

species a group of living things that are very similar   4

Index

Further Readings

Greenaway, Frank. *Eyewitness Junior's Amazing Bats.* Alfred A. Knopf, 1991.

Halton, Cheryl Mays. *Those Amazing Bats.* Dillon Press, 1991.

Hume, Rob. *Bird Watching.* Random House, 1993.